THE IMPACT OF ENVIRONMENTALISM:

FOOD AND FARMING

Jen Green

www.raintreepublishers.co.uk
Visit our website to find out
more information about
Raintree books.

To order:
☎ Phone 0845 6044371
▤ Fax +44 (0) 1865 312263
▣ Email myorders@raintreepublishers.co.uk

Customers from outside the UK please telephone +44 1865 312262

Raintree is an imprint of Capstone Global Library
Limited, a company incorporated in England and
Wales having its registered office at 7 Pilgrim Street,
London, EC4V 6LB – Registered company number:
6695582

Text © Capstone Global Library Limited 2013
First published in hardback in 2013
The moral rights of the proprietor have been asserted.

Edited by Andrew Farrow, Adam Miller, and
    Diyan Leake
Designed by Victoria Allen
Picture research by Elizabeth Alexander
Illustrations by Oxford Designers & Illustrators
Originated by Capstone Global Library Ltd
Printed and bound in China by Leo Paper Products Ltd

ISBN 978 1 406 23859 4
16 15 14 13 12
10 9 8 7 6 5 4 3 2 1

British Library Cataloguing in Publication Data
A full catalogue record for this book is available from
the British Library.

Acknowledgements
The author and publisher are grateful to the following
for permission to reproduce copyright material:
Alamy pp. 15 (© Steve Morgan), 29 (© FLPA), 41
(© Jon Arnold Images Ltd), 49 (© Nik Wheeler); Corbis
pp. 7 (Mark Malijan/Demotix), 9, 11 (Reuters/K.K.
Arora), 12 (Andy Aitchison), 25 (Gerd Ludwig), 35,
45 (Ecoscence/Sally A. Morgan); Getty Images pp.
19 (Rodrigo Baleia/LatinContent), 31 (The Christian
Science Monitor/John Nordell), 39 (Ariel Skelley),
43 (Bloomberg/Daniel Acker), 52 (AFP/Roberto
Schmidt); Photolibrary pp. 33 (Peter Arnold Images/
Luiz C. Marigo); Shutterstock pp. 20 (© Walter G.
Arce), 23 (© Grisha), 27 (© FotoVeto), 37 (© Norman
Chan), 47 (© Frontpage), 55 (© Lane V. Erickson), 57
(© paparazzit); SuperStock p. 51 (© Nomad).

Cover photograph of (top) chickens inside cages,
reproduced with permission of Corbis (© Robert
Benson/Aurora Photos), and (bottom) chickens
standing in field, reproduced with permission of
SuperStock (© OJO Images).

Every effort has been made to contact copyright
holders of material reproduced in this book. Any
omissions will be rectified in subsequent printings if
notice is given to the publisher.

Disclaimer
All the internet addresses (URLs) given in this book
were valid at the time of going to press. However, due
to the dynamic nature of the internet, some addresses
may have changed, or sites may have changed or
ceased to exist since publication. While the author and
publisher regret any inconvenience this may cause
readers, no responsibility for any such changes can be
accepted by either the author or the publisher.

CONTENTS

Thinking about food sources 4

What is environmentalism? 6

Modernization of farming 8

The impact of farming 16

The "greening" of farming 26

The food industry 36

Feast and famine..............................44

Looking into the future 52

Timeline......................................58

Glossary 60

Find out more 62

Index 64

Words printed in **bold** are explained in the Glossary.

THINKING ABOUT FOOD SOURCES

Think about all the foods you have eaten today. Perhaps you started the day with cereals, fruit juice, and toast, or even a cooked breakfast. In the course of a day, most of us living in the **developed world** consume a huge range of different foods. Almost all of the food we eat is grown by farmers, including fruits and vegetables, eggs, meat and dairy produce, and grains such as wheat and oats, which are used to make bread, cereal, and pasta. Even fish and shellfish, traditionally captured from the wild, are nowadays often farmed. In addition, the world's farmers also supply us with wool, cotton, rubber, and many other products.

Where does our food come from?

In developed countries, most of the food we eat comes from supermarkets that source it from farms, plantations, and ranches all over the world. Nowadays, food production is a truly global business, and the traders and supermarkets that control the global industry are immensely powerful. In the last 20 years or so, environmentalism, or "green thinking", has had a big influence on the way we think about food and what foods we buy.

Environmentalists have set people thinking about the impact of farming and food production on the natural world – for example, the loss of wild **habitats** caused by the spread of agriculture, and the harmful effects of pollutants such as **pesticides**. But how much has the environmental movement actually changed the way we farm and produce food? Read on to find out.

Changing times

Thirty years ago, relatively few shoppers thought much about where their food came from or whether farming harmed the environment. Now we are much more likely to scrutinize labels that list ingredients and state where foods were grown or sourced. People are now more likely to buy foods grown locally than they were a decade ago. More people are buying foods that have been grown **organically**, without using chemicals, or choosing brands that offer growers a fair price. We are more likely to think about whether the fish we buy is scarce or abundant. All this is down to environmentalism. In addition, environmental scientists are now working with governments, farmers, and food producers to reduce the harmful effect of agriculture on the natural world.

Thinking about food and farming

Think again about the food you have eaten today. Most people in developed countries such as the United Kingdom, the United States, and Australia get enough to eat, with a diet that contains a good balance of **nutrients**. In less developed regions such as Africa, many people eat just one meal per day, and have a very limited diet that does not meet their nutritional needs.

This map shows some of the places discussed in environmental case studies in this book.

WHAT IS ENVIRONMENTALISM?

Environmentalism, also known as the green movement, is the movement to protect the natural world from the impact of human activities. Environmentalists work to improve the quality of the air, water, and soil and to protect Earth's **biodiversity** – the variety of living things. They also seek to change economies, government policies, and people's lifestyles so that human needs for natural resources are met without damaging the planet.

Environmentalists use a wide range of methods to achieve their aims. For example, they may **lobby** governments to pass new laws to protect the environment. Or they may campaign to inform the public about environmental issues.

Green organizations

The green movement includes international organizations, government bodies, small groups, and individuals. The green movement is about attitudes and lifestyles, rather than being linked to particular professions, so people from all walks of life are environmentalists. The movement also includes people with a wide range of views, including conservationists who work to preserve natural resources for human use, and people who are sometimes called "deep greens", who believe that nature should be protected for its own sake. Most environmentalists work within the law, but a small number of activists believe that illegal actions are justified to highlight practices they believe harm the environment, such as testing **genetically modified (GM)** crops.

The rise of environmentalism

The environmental movement began in the 19th century, when naturalists and thinkers began to campaign to protect the wild places of Europe and North America from development. This resulted in the creation of the first national parks and reserves. Early in the 20th century, environmentalists worked to publicize the harmful effects of air, water, and soil pollution. Many countries passed laws to reduce pollution.

Following the creation of the United Nations (UN) in 1945, international bodies such as the International Union for Conservation of Nature (IUCN) were set up to protect the environment. Another UN agency, the Food and Agriculture Organization (FAO), was formed to improve world food production and promote good farming practices.

In the 1970s, environmental groups such as Greenpeace, Friends of the Earth, and the World Wildlife Fund became known internationally for their campaigns to protect wildlife and nature. In the 1980s, environmentalists developed the idea of **sustainability** – managing Earth's resources to meet our present needs while preserving those resources for the future.

Global warming

In the late 1970s and 1980s, scientists found convincing evidence that human activities are increasing the temperature of the Earth's climate. The change has been caused by increased levels of **greenhouse gases**, such as carbon dioxide and methane in the air, partly due to **deforestation** and the burning of fossil fuels. If the **global warming** continued, environmentalists warned, climates would change and polar ice would start to melt, producing rising sea levels.

The world's nations met to try to agree reductions in greenhouse gases, but this has proved difficult. Environmentalists are also campaigning for a shift to **renewable** energies that do not produce greenhouse gases, and have convinced many people to use energy more carefully.

In 2009, environmentalists at the World Climate Conference highlighted the effect of global warming on wildlife such as the giant panda. Thirty thousand demonstrators took part in protests.

MODERNIZATION OF FARMING

Farming is the world's oldest profession, dating back over 11,000 years. In the last 200 years, farming in many parts of the world has been transformed from a labour-intensive industry into a highly scientific and commercial global operation. However, environmentalists have shown that many changes in farming harm the natural world.

The origins of farming

Around 9000 BC, people in the Middle East discovered that wild strains of plants could be cultivated for their edible seeds. They began to keep animals such as sheep, goats, and cattle for their milk, meat, and hides, and later to irrigate the land using water drawn from rivers. This was the start of farming, and it led people to abandon a nomadic lifestyle, hunting and gathering wild foods, and settle in one place. Settlements sprang up and civilization began.

By 6000 BC, farming had developed in other regions, including Egypt, China, India, and Mexico. A simple plough called an ard was invented some time between 4000 and 3000 BC. By 3500 BC, metal-tipped ploughs were being pulled by oxen.

Early farming techniques

By 500 BC, Roman farmers were specializing in growing wheat, keeping vines, or rearing dairy cattle. Some Roman farmers practiced **crop rotation**, varying the crops grown in fields to improve the soil. These advances spread through much of the Roman Empire by AD 200.

Farming changed relatively little for hundreds of years. Farmers followed a yearly round of preparing the soil, planting, weeding, harvesting, and storing crops. Each of these tasks was done by hand or with the aid of draft animals, involving days or weeks of hard work.

The Agricultural Revolution

In the 1700s a period of innovation called the **Agricultural Revolution** began. In 1701, the mechanical **seed drill** was invented. This horse-drawn device ploughed a groove called a furrow and dropped seeds into it. Other machinery, such as the mechanical reaper to cut crops such as wheat, followed in the early 1800s. By the mid-1800s steam-powered traction engines were hauling farm equipment in North America and Europe. The first petrol- and diesel-driven tractors appeared in the 1920s. Within 20 years the new machinery had replaced horses and many workers on farms.

By the early 1900s, the pioneering work of Austrian scientist Gregor Mendel had led to a greater understanding of genetics, which allowed farmers to develop more productive crops and livestock through selective breeding – choosing the best stock to breed from. By the 1930s, electricity was widespread on farms in the United States and Europe, greatly reducing the labour involved in routine chores.

Then and Now
Harvest time

In the mid-19th century, it took a dozen farmhands working all day to harvest grain in a 2-hectare (5-acre) field. The crop still had to be **threshed** to separate the stalks, and **winnowed** to remove the chaff – many more hours of labour. Following the development of the mechanical reaper in the 1840s and the reaper-binder in the 1930s, combine harvesters appeared. One farm worker driving a modern combine will take just an hour to harvest 2 hectares of wheat and process the grain.

Early combine harvesters were pulled by teams of horses, as in this wheat harvest in Oregon, USA. After World War II, tractors replaced horses on farms across the developed world.

Farm chemicals

In the early 1900s, scientific understanding of the nutrients required by crops led to the development of artificial fertilizers using fossil fuels. These greatly increased productivity. Scientists also developed farm pesticides – herbicides to kill weeds, fungicides to destroy moulds, and insecticides to control insect pests.

Bumper crops

By the 1950s, the world's population was rising quickly. Farmers were under pressure to produce more crops to meet the growing demand for food. During the 1940s and 1950s, scientists in the United States, Western Europe, and Australia developed new highly productive strains of wheat, maize, and rice, known as **high-yield varieties (HYVs)**.

Increasing mechanization, HYVs, and other technology meant that many farms were now commercial enterprises rather than small-scale family businesses. This was because only relatively large farms could afford the cost of the machinery, fertilizers, and other inputs. The drive to increase productivity led many farms to specialize in growing the same crop year after year, a practice known as **monoculture**. The most successful farms were now run **intensively**, with farmers investing heavily in inputs such as seeds, machinery, and chemicals to produce high yields. Fewer farms in developed countries were run in the old way, with a low investment per hectare to produce a lower yield – a method known as **extensive farming**.

Then and Now
Changing US farms

In the 1850s, most farms in the United States were small farms run by families who grew crops and raised a few cattle, sheep, and chickens. Farming was the main occupation, but these small farms produced only enough food for the family. This is called **subsistence farming**. Some 150 years later, just 3 per cent of the US population is employed in farming, but most farms are large-scale businesses providing food for more than 100 people.

By the 1950s, HYVs were doubling or even trebling yields in the developed world. The use of technology and equipment such as greenhouses meant that intensive farmers were less at the mercy of weather and climate.

The "Green Revolution"

Farms in less developed regions such as Africa and Asia were far less productive, and famine was widespread. In the 1960s, HYVs were introduced to less developed parts of the world. This was known as the **Green Revolution**, and the results were spectacular. India and Pakistan, which had suffered terrible famines in the 1960s, became self-sufficient in food during the 1970s.

HYVs were hailed as "miracle crops", and the companies that produced them confidently predicted the end of world hunger. Environmentalists, however, were concerned that the Green Revolution was far from green in terms of its effects on the environment. HYVs relied on the use of chemical pesticides and fertilizers, which environmentalists believed were harming natural **ecosystems**. They were also reducing biodiversity – the variety of plants and animals in a habitat.

HYVs were also only effective on well-watered or irrigated land, which was overstretching water supplies in dry regions. What is more, HYVs required heavy investment in seeds, chemicals, and technology. This favoured larger-scale farmers in Africa and India, but forced many small farmers into debt and out of business.

In developing countries such as India, many farms are still not mechanized. These villagers are threshing a rice crop by hand.

Global food markets

A great many of the foods we buy in Western supermarkets come from economically developing countries in the tropics, where they are grown for export. Many of these countries were once European colonies. Before and during colonial times, highly productive crops from around the world were introduced to other regions. For example, bananas, originally found in Asia, were introduced to the Caribbean, South America, and West Africa. In the 18th and 19th centuries, crops grown in colonies provided cheap foods and other raw materials, such as cotton and rubber, for the colonial powers of Europe.

Cash crops – who benefits?

Today the governments of many former colonies encourage the growing of **cash crops** for export, because the money helps them to develop their economies. However, the supermarkets and food-processing companies based in the developed world that buy the produce are immensely powerful. They drive down the prices offered to growers so that they can offer Western shoppers cheap food. Growers in developing countries get very low prices for their produce, with many farm workers earning less than £1 a day. Growers are also at the mercy of changing world prices. For example, the average price of bananas in the United Kingdom dropped by more than half between 1997 and 2008.

A coffee grower in Uganda spreads out coffee beans to dry. Her crop is sold through a fair trade organization.

Food justice

Since the 1970s, environmental groups such as Friends of the Earth have joined aid agencies such as Oxfam in calling for "food justice" – a fairer deal for growers in less developed countries. The **fair trade movement** is part of this. Green organizations also highlight the harmful environmental impact of cash-crop farming.

In some developing countries, so much land is taken over for cash-crop agriculture that little room is left for subsistence farming. Growing just one or two cash crops means that poor countries are at great risk of crop disease and insect plague. They can be very badly hit by drought and other natural disasters. In 1998, for example, Hurricane Mitch devastated the banana crop on several Caribbean islands, which provided much of their country's income. Environmentalists and aid organizations encourage farmers in developing countries to diversify their agriculture, with the aim of becoming more self-sufficient in food and less dependent on the ups and downs of international trade.

Fair trade

Launched in the 1980s, fair trade is a movement that aims to give growers in less developed countries a fair price for produce such as tropical fruits, tea, coffee, cocoa, rubber, and cotton. Fair trade growers have to meet strict environmental standards to ensure that their methods do not harm the natural world. In return they receive a guaranteed price that does not change with world trade. The money is used to improve living standards, to fund community projects, and improve technology. In recent years, campaigns such as Friends of the Earth's Real Food Campaign have helped to publicize the idea of fair trade to Western shoppers. Thanks to the movement's popularity, a growing number of outlets stock an increasingly wide range of fair trade goods.

ENVIRONMENTALISM IN ACTION

The GM debate

Since the 1970s, advances in **biotechnology** have allowed scientists to transfer **genes** from one species to another. Genes are chemicals within cells that control inheritance. They allow traits, such as the colour and size of fruit, or the ability to resist disease, to pass from one generation to the next. This science is **genetic engineering**, and the living things that are altered are called **genetically modified organisms (GMOs)**.

The purpose of GMOs

By adding genes from one organism to another, scientists have modified crops such as tomatoes to look or taste better, or stay fresh for longer. Crops such as soybeans and maize have been changed to resist insect pests or herbicides, so that farmers can spray their crops fewer times and save money. Biotech companies say that GM crops can play a major role in reducing world hunger. They say that creating crops that need to be sprayed fewer times is good for nature. Environmental groups say that more testing is needed before we can be sure they will not harm the natural world. They also point out that GM crops are doing little, if anything, to relieve world hunger.

A stormy debate

In the 1990s, environmental groups such as Greenpeace launched campaigns to publicize the potential dangers of GMOs. They argued that the long-term impact of GMOs needed to be more carefully assessed before they were widely introduced. Some environmentalists were even against testing GM crops in the open, since they believed that pollen from GMOs could spread to "contaminate" nearby crops. In 1998, this fear was realized in the United Kingdom when pollen from a GM rapeseed trial spread to contaminate a rapeseed crop in a nearby field. Some scientists voiced fears that GM crops might crossbreed with weeds to create "superweeds" that could resist herbicides and so spread unchecked. In 1999, Greenpeace supporters in the United Kingdom took action. They trespassed on to private land and destroyed test fields of GM maize.

The biotech companies argue that genetic engineering is only an extension of the selective breeding techniques that farmers had practiced for centuries to improve crops and livestock.

Where are GM foods sold?

In most of Europe, New Zealand, and Australia, campaigns by environmental groups convinced many people that GM crops were unsafe. A 2001 poll found that 70 per cent of Europeans did not want to eat GM food. Crop trials were halted, and supermarkets in the United Kingdom banned GM products, fearing that consumers would boycott their stores if they sold GM foods. However, in the United States, Canada, and some other countries, GM crops have gone ahead.

In 2011, environmental groups such as GM Watch increased pressure on the US government to introduce legislation requiring all GM foods to be labelled. In the European Union, Australia, and New Zealand, products containing more than 1 per cent of GM food have to be clearly labelled, but not in the United States and Canada, where most crops are now modified.

In the summer of 1999, Greenpeace activists destroyed a test field of GM maize to publicize the potential danger of GM trials contaminating nearby crops.

THE IMPACT OF FARMING

Improvements in agriculture over the last 50 years or so have greatly increased world food production. However, there has been clear and increasing evidence that intensive farming methods have often harmed natural ecosystems and the air, water, and soil.

Disappearing habitats

For over 10,000 years, farmers have been clearing natural habitats to plant crops. According to the United Nations, farmland now covers 38 per cent of the world's land area, and half of all habitable land. The conversion of wild ecosystems such as grasslands, forests, and wetlands to agriculture is a major cause of habitat loss. Extinctions are happening at 100–1,000 times the natural rate, and habitat loss is one of the causes.

Expanding farmlands

In the last 200 years, habitat loss due to agriculture has increased as human populations have grown. Just a few centuries ago, vast swathes of wild grassland covered the North American prairies and the Russian **steppes**. In the 19th and 20th centuries, these wild "seas of grass" were ploughed up to grow wheat and maize, or converted to cattle pasture.

Recent examples of habitat loss include the clearance of the Brazilian grasslands for soybean cultivation, and the destruction of Indonesia's rainforests for oil palm plantations. Many rare species are now endangered.

Population growth

Environmental scientists predict that as human populations continue to grow in the next 50 years (perhaps to 9 billion by 2040), farmlands will continue to expand. The WWF predicts that another 120 million hectares (296 million acres) of land will be put under cultivation during this time in rapidly developing countries. This land will include habitats rich in biodiversity, such as rainforests and marshes.

Conserving habitats

Since the early days of conservation in the 19th century, environmentalists such as US naturalist John Muir (1838–1914) have been concerned about the loss of wild areas to agriculture and other developments.

Muir campaigned for the creation of the first national parks in the United States from the 1870s. Countries around the world followed America's lead, and today there are more than 37,000 parks and reserves worldwide.

Environmental groups still see the creation of reserves and parks as the most effective way of protecting ecosystems and wildlife. However, groups such as WWF also believe that much can be done to make farmlands more **eco-friendly** (supportive to wildlife).

Then and Now
Hedge destruction

Traditional farmlands where a variety of crops are grown can provide important habitats for wild plants, fungi, soil-dwelling insects, and larger animals. In the early 1900s, the British countryside was a patchwork of small fields divided by hedges, planted since the 18th century to provide shelter for crops and prevent erosion. However, between 1945 and 1990, one-third of those hedges were destroyed to create bigger fields. European farmers are now encouraged to replant hedges and conserve ancient hedges.

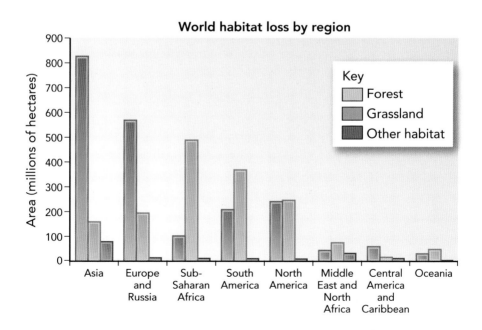

This table shows destruction to forests, grasslands, and other global habitat loss by region by the year 2000.

ENVIRONMENTALISM IN ACTION

Farming and ranching in the Amazon rainforest

The Amazon rainforest is one of Earth's most biodiverse habitats, home to at least one-tenth of all plant and animal species that have been identified to date. It is also home to hundreds of forest peoples, some of whom traditionally cleared small areas of forest to cultivate crops and then moved on, allowing the forest to regrow.

Forest destruction

Since the 1970s, environmentalists have warned that the rainforests of Brazil were fast disappearing. In 1970, the Brazilian rainforest covered 4 million square kilometers (1.5 million square miles); in 2008 that figure was down to 3.3 million (1.3 million). Despite protests from conservationists, deforestation has accelerated in the 21st century.

Why are Brazilian rainforests being destroyed?

Brazilian deforestation is partly caused by hardwood logging. Forests are felled to make way for new settlements, hydroelectric schemes, mines, roads, and airstrips – but, above all, to clear land for commercial farming and ranching. Brazil is a major producer of beef, so cattle ranches occupy 80 per cent of all deforested land. Most of these ranches are owned by multinational companies that supply beef to North America. Increasing amounts of land are also being cleared for soybean cultivation. This crop is grown to feed livestock, and also for **biofuel**. Farming is intensive and, because rainforest land is naturally low in nutrients, there is heavy use of artificial fertilizers to prevent the soil from becoming exhausted.

Protecting the Amazon

Deforestation in Brazilian rainforests destroys incredibly rich ecosystems and harms local peoples. It also impacts on regional and global weather patterns. Since the 1970s and 1980s, environmental groups such as WWF and Greenpeace have campaigned to halt forest destruction. In 1987, the US-based Rainforest Action Network (RAN) organized such a campaign.

They asked consumers to boycott the fast-food chain Burger King, which was importing cheap beef from tropical forests, including the Amazon. After sales dropped by 12 per cent, the chain cancelled contracts for rainforest beef, providing an important example of how action by consumers in the developed world could help to preserve distant ecosystems.

In the early 2000s, Greenpeace noted that only 8 per cent of the world's ancient forests were under strict protection. Together with other groups, they called for the governments of rainforest nations to establish a global network of protected areas and to ban all new industrialized logging until a plan for rainforest conservation could be drawn up. They put pressure on governments to crack down on illegal logging, and canvassed supporters to raise the huge funds needed to set up and manage the new reserves.

Environmental groups also work with food manufacturers, retailers, and timber merchants in the developed world to ensure that their business practices are not linked to deforestation. In 2009, after pressure from environmental groups, four of the world's largest commercial beef customers agreed not to buy beef from newly deforested land – a significant victory for conservation in the Amazon.

A field in the Mato Grosso area of the Amazon is prepared for soybeans. This region in south-west Brazil has suffered a particularly high rate of deforestation. It lost 48 per cent of its forest in a single year, 2003–2004.

Fertilizers

In the last 50 years, scientists have learned that chemicals used in farming, known as **agrochemicals**, can lead to pollution and harm wildlife. Artificial fertilizers are widely used in farming to add nutrients to the soil. Their use doubled following the introduction of HYVs in the 1960s. However, nutrients not absorbed by plants drain away into streams and rivers, where they fertilize the water. This causes the rapid growth of algae and bacteria that blanket the surface and remove oxygen, killing fish and other wildlife. This problem is called **eutrophication**.

Following environmental studies, national laws and international agreements have been introduced to help limit chemical pollution. However, it is still common in wetlands bordering farmlands.

Problem pesticides

Scientists estimate that weeds, disease, and insects reduce the world's food production by up to 40 per cent. Chemical pesticides are used to reduce crop losses and produce unblemished fruits and vegetables. However, these poisons can enter water supplies and food chains and kill not only pests but also useful organisms, such as worms that keep the soil healthy, and bees and butterflies that pollinate plants. They can also enter the water supply and food chain. Since the 1960s, environmentalists have warned of the dangers of using pesticides (see box).

A plane dusts crops with insecticide. Such practices result in pollution of nearby waterways. Studies show that 100 per cent of all surface waters in the United States contain traces of pesticides.

Despite this, pesticide use increased at least 30 times worldwide between 1950 and the end of the 1980s. However, pests develop immunity to the poison over time, and more powerful chemicals must be used in greater quantities. Fortunately for farmland ecosystems, scientists are now developing pesticides that are less harmful to the environment – for example, insecticides that target insect pests but do not harm "helpful" insects. Organic pesticides that are safe for pets and wildlife, and break down on contact with the soil, have become increasingly popular. Other measures include introducing natural predators of pests, such as ladybirds (see page 30).

Then and Now
DDT

During the 1950s, farmers around the world began to use a powerful new pesticide called DDT. However, in 1962 US biologist Rachel Carson published a book called *Silent Spring*, describing the environmental impacts of DDT. Carson's work for the US Fish and Wildlife Service had produced overwhelming evidence that DDT was affecting many kinds of wildlife through food chains. The poison was absorbed by small creatures such as mice and insects, which provided food for predators such as hawks and eagles. It was also causing birds of prey to lay eggs with weak shells that broke easily.

Silent Spring became an international bestseller. It inspired thousands of people to join conservation groups. It also led to the creation of the US Environmental Protection Agency in 1970. Following detailed studies, DDT was banned in the United States in 1972, and in much of Europe in the 1980s. In 2004, the Stockholm Convention outlawed its use in farming.

However, DDT is still used to control mosquitoes that carry the disease malaria, which kills around 780,000 people each year. This causes debate among scientists, health experts, and environmentalists as to whether it is more important to protect lives or the environment. Farmers in countries such as India and North Korea also continue to use it. The World Health Organization (WHO) estimates that 200,000 people die every year through improper use of DDT and other pesticides.

Overuse of water

Crops cannot grow without water. Where rainfall is scarce or erratic, farmers must irrigate their fields using ditches, canals, pumps, and (more recently) sprinkler systems. Since the mid-1900s, intensive farming and the introduction of thirsty HYVs have increased water use. Over-extraction is now stretching global water supplies, with major food-producing nations such as the United States, China, India, and Australia all reporting **depleted** reserves. According to the US Environmental Protection Agency, water consumption increased six-fold in the 20th century, with 70 per cent of all fresh water being used in agriculture globally.

As a result, rivers and lakes in many parts of the world are regularly running low, or dry, or shrinking. Groundwater sources, known as **aquifers**, are also being depleted. Still worse, environmental groups such as WWF report that up to 60 per cent of water used in agriculture – 1,500 trillion litres (400 million gallons) per year – is being wasted through evaporation, leaks, over-watering, or growing unsuitable crops.

Shrinking lakes

Over the past 50 years, some of the world's largest lakes have been severely depleted by overuse of water. Lake Chad in Africa was once the world's sixth-largest lake. In years of plentiful rainfall in the 1950s, it covered 26,000 square kilometres (10,000 square miles), but has since been heavily depleted by drought and agriculture. By 2000, it covered just 2,500 square kilometres (965 square miles). Experts fear it may disappear altogether by 2100.

Salinization

Overwatering can make the ground waterlogged. Evaporation can also cause natural salts in the soil to rise to the surface, making the soil too salty for farming. This is called **salinization**, and it is a major problem in hot countries where evaporation is high. In Iran and Egypt, up to one-half of all arable land is affected by salinization.

Irrigation is a major cause of water wastage. Huge amounts of water evaporate from reservoirs, canals, and sprinkler systems.

What can be done?

Problems of over-extraction and salinization can be countered by better management of water resources. Environmental scientists advise using more efficient irrigating techniques, such as drip-feeding, which supplies water direct to plant roots and so reduces evaporation. Farmers can also switch to crops that need less water and can tolerate higher salt levels. Scientists in Israel have developed salt-tolerant melons, vines, and tomatoes.

Harming the soil

Soil is a precious resource for farmers. Yet badly managed farming can quickly destroy or degrade soil. In wild ecosystems, the roots of trees and plants bind the soil together. As farmlands expand, grasslands are ploughed up, and forests are felled, these root systems are removed. This leaves soil vulnerable to erosion, so that heavy rain can wash it away.

Experts report that soybean farming in Brazil results in the loss of 56 million tonnes of topsoil annually. In farmlands bordering dry areas, overgrazing by farm animals can remove vegetation, causing deserts to expand. This is called **desertification**. Environmental scientists estimate that up to one-third of all arable land has been destroyed by erosion and poor farming practices since 1960.

Modern livestock farming

Farmers have been raising livestock such as cattle, sheep, pigs, and poultry for over 10,000 years. In the 20th century, livestock farming became industrialized in many areas of the world. All stock farmers must meet their animals' needs for food and shelter, and look after their health.

Housing

On many commercial stock farms, animals are kept indoors, often in cramped pens and cages that restrict their movements. Environmentalists and other groups criticize this method, which they call factory farming. On battery farms, poultry reared to produce eggs are kept indoors in small wire cages, with as many as 10,000 hens stacked in tiers. Pigs are kept in pens in fattening houses.

In the United States, some cattle are kept in **feedlots** where they never see grass. In other countries, such as Australia, sheep and cattle herds range freely on ranches that can cover 10,000 square kilometres (3,900 square miles) or more. But overall, far fewer stock range freely on ranches – and meat from these ranches is generally more expensive than the factory-produced meat.

Feeding and breeding

Intensively farmed animals are fed on concentrates that contain an exact mix of high-protein nutrients. Their feed often contains **antibiotics** to fight infection, and chemical **hormones** to stimulate growth. Intensive farms are highly mechanized, with automated systems such as conveyer belts delivering food, removing waste, and collecting eggs.

The use of technology and chemicals in modern livestock farming has greatly increased production, allowing farmers to deliver cheap food. In developed countries such as the United States, livestock farm outputs have more than doubled since the early 1900s.

Animal welfare groups criticize factory farming for providing a very poor quality of life for livestock, arguing that intensive methods cause the animals measurable stress and even pain. Environmental groups highlight the damage to the environment.

Criticisms of factory farming

In a 2004 report, Friends of the Earth summarized the harmful effects of intensive farming:

- Commercial farms produce vast quantities of animal waste that can contaminate water and soil through leaks and run-off. Nitrogen in the waste causes a reduction in oxygen in the water, which harms aquatic life.
- The farming of crops such as soybeans for fodder involves deforestation and high use of chemicals, resulting in pollution, habitat loss, and reduced biodiversity.
- Increased mechanization on stock farms reduces numbers of farm workers and keeps farm wages low. Many small farms have been forced out of business by large-scale farms.
- The high use of energy in factory farming and fodder cultivation contributes to greenhouse gas emissions. In addition, raising huge numbers of cattle adds methane and nitrous oxide to the atmosphere – both very powerful greenhouse gases.
- Overuse of antibiotics in intensive farming can encourage the appearance of new strains of disease-causing organisms, such as strains of the bacteria E.coli.
- Intensive livestock rearing can lead to loss of genetic diversity, as fewer breeds are being reared.

Some 85,000 cattle are reared in feedlots on this intensive stock farm in the south-western United States.

THE "GREENING" OF FARMING

Since the 1970s and 1980s, green campaigners have drawn attention to the harmful effects of industrialized farming on the environment. Green activists have put pressure on governments, farmers, and food producers to reduce pollution from farming. Green thinking is starting to influence government polices and farming practices. It is also influencing the choices we make as shoppers and the way we live our lives.

European farming policies

The Common Agricultural Policy (CAP) was developed shortly after the founding of the European Economic Community, now the European Union (EU), in 1957. The aim was to modernize European farming and increase productivity in order to make Europe self-sufficient in food. Through payments called **subsidies**, CAP encouraged farmers to switch to intensive methods with increased mechanization, technology, and use of pesticides and fertilizers. Hedges were removed to enlarge fields to make them more productive, and small farms combined to make larger ones. However, environmental groups were highly critical of CAP. In 2004, Friends of the Earth stated: "Intensive farming methods are the product of government farming policies of the last 50 years. We need a new system that supports farmers who protect wildlife and gives them a fair price for their food".

Green reforms

By 1990, CAP measures were so successful that Europe was not only self-sufficient in food, but producing surpluses of many products. Environmental groups such as Greenpeace and WWF called for CAP to be reformed, to allow farmers to work in ways that would be more in tune with the environment. Environmentally sensitive schemes such as the UK's Countryside Stewardship Scheme were introduced throughout the EU. Under these schemes, farmers were paid to restore farmland ecosystems through measures such as replanting woodlands and hedges, and leaving areas of uncultivated land, called set-aside, to encourage wildlife.

Grants were offered to farmers to conserve landscapes rich in biodiversity, such as chalk downlands, hay meadows, coastal dunes, and moorlands. The aim was to halt the decline of wildlife such as birds on arable land by providing habitats and food, especially during winter. Similar schemes were introduced in the United States, Canada, Australia, and other countries, to promote farming methods that were more sustainable and kinder to nature.

Then and Now
Farming with birds in mind

Hope Farm in Cambridgeshire was purchased by the Royal Society for the Protection of Birds (RSPB) in 1999. Before the conservation group took over, this small arable farm of 180 hectares (444 acres) was worked intensively, with heavy use of machinery and chemicals helping to maximize profits. The RSPB conducted a two-year survey of birds and other wildlife and decided to farm the land using modern methods, but reducing chemicals. A wider range of crops was planted, and hedges were restored to provide food and shelter for birds. Since 1999, the farm has yielded lower profits than the RSPB had projected, but numbers and variety of birdlife are increasing, bucking the general trend of decline of birds on farms.

Birds that live in English hedges, such as the yellowhammer (*Emberiza citrinella*), are generally in decline on farmland, but environmentally friendly practices can help to halt this trend.

ENVIRONMENTALISM IN ACTION

The Environmental Stewardship Scheme

The Environmental Stewardship Scheme (ESS) was launched in the United Kingdom in 2005. Managed by Natural England, a government body, the ESS aims to conserve wildlife and biodiversity, safeguard natural resources, maintain traditional features of the landscape, and conserve historic sites. In contracts lasting five to ten years, farmers are paid per hectare (2.47 acres) to farm in ways that support the environment. The scheme has several different levels, including one strand for organic farmers (see pages 30–31). The programme also aims to improve water quality, provide flood management, and reduce erosion. Another goal is to encourage general understanding of the countryside among both local people and visitors.

Supporting wildlife

Perching Manor Farm in Sussex covers 615 hectares (1,500 acres) of countryside, of which two-thirds is rare chalk upland on the South Downs. The remainder is lowland fields at the foot of the Downs, where the soil is clay. Traditionally, the farm was mainly arable, though sheep were also grazed. Like most UK farms, Perching Manor was farmed intensively in the late 20th century, with extensive use of farm chemicals and machinery.

In around 1990, in a previous government scheme, the farmer was paid to grass over the previously cultivated chalk upland. It was believed that grassland would provide a better habitat for birds and other wildlife. However, environmental experts later realized that arable land under low-impact cultivation (which means using environmentally sensitive methods) would in fact sustain a greater variety of birds and other species than a relatively barren covering of grass.

ESS in action

Under the ESS, some of the chalk upland was ploughed up in 2010. Cereal crops were planted non-intensively and without using chemicals. The aim was to provide a harvestable crop, but also food, habitats, and nesting sites for birds. Areas of grassland were left uncultivated to support wildlife and also protect historic sites, such as the remains of a medieval village. A 500-metre (1,640-foot) beetle bank was planted to encourage natural predators of pests, and so reduce the need for insecticides in nearby farmland.

The lowland fields are farmed more intensively, but careful consideration is given to the use of agrochemicals and artificial fertilizers, which are used to maximize crop yields. Field borders are left as wildlife corridors, and some fields converted to pasture. A small woodland was coppiced (cut back) and selectively cleared to provide habitats for woodland life, such as deer and songbirds. The farmer now plans to shift to a more mixed pattern of farming, with the introduction of cattle as well as sheep.

Farm manager David Ellin explained: "The aim is to produce a patchwork of arable land rather than a 'green concrete' grassland which does not really benefit downland birds and other wildlife". The scheme has already yielded results. For example, the chalk upland now supports some rare species of grassland birds.

Hedges and strips of uncultivated land around the edges of fields provide a refuge for insects, birds, mice, and other wildlife.

Organic farming

Thanks to environmental groups, most people are now aware of the costs to nature of intensive farming. Many people are concerned about the harmful effects of farm chemicals, both on the natural world and on human health. Environmental groups are now campaigning for food to be grown in ways that are more sustainable – that provide healthy, nutritious food without damaging the environment.

Organic farming is one method of sustainable farming. It involves growing food and rearing livestock using more natural methods, and without chemicals. Farmers have to follow strict rules for their produce to be certified as organic.

Organic methods

Organic arable farmers use a variety of methods to improve soil quality without artificial fertilizers. For example, organic farmers use crop waste, manure, or even seaweed to fertilize fields. They also practice crop rotation, growing different crops often in a four-year cycle. At least one year in every four, fields are left **fallow** (uncultivated), or the farmer plants a **legume** crop such as peas or beans, which returns nitrogen to the soil.

To control pests, many organic farmers use a system called Integrated Pest Management (IPM). This involves using natural predators, such as ladybirds, to control pests like aphids. Farmers may leave field borders wild to encourage these predators. Growing a variety of crops also helps to control pests, since crop-eating insects such as aphids and locusts multiply on farms where their favourite food plants are grown year after year. The practice of **intercropping** can also reduce pest numbers. This is when farmers plant several crops in rows, often including varieties such as onions, that discourage pests.

Organic livestock farmers do not add hormones or antibiotics to animal feed. Many also allow their animals to range freely. Since the 1990s, the variety of free-range and organic produce has increased dramatically, and these foods have become much more widely available.

> "Organic farming benefits people and nature. It is essential for conserving biodiversity … it supports rural development, fair trade, food safety, and animal welfare."
>
> WWF

Pros and cons of organic farming

Between 2001 and 2004, the number of certified organic farmers in the United Kingdom rose from 2,500 to 4,100. But is organic farming really the best solution for the environment? Here are some pros and cons:

Advantages

Organic farming is widely accepted as being better for nature. Environmentalists point out that not using chemicals reduces input costs for farmers, which favours small-scale farms. They say organic farming uses less water, and so reduces the pressure on rivers, lakes, and aquifers. Many shoppers are convinced that food grown without chemicals is healthier and also tastes better.

Disadvantages

Organic farming also has its drawbacks. Critics point out that because organic farming produces lower yields, the food is more expensive. In the 1990s, organic foods were very popular, but since 2008, economic recession has reduced demand. In addition, critics say that organic farming takes up more land to produce the same amount of food, which would put pressure on wild habitats if all current food production was produced organically.

An organic farmer in the eastern United States carries a box of green cabbages. Farmers have to meet rigorous standards to win organic accreditation.

ENVIRONMENTALISM IN ACTION

Sustainable forestry in the Amazon

In the Amazon rainforest, a type of farming called **agroforestry** is providing an alternative to the cycle of clearing and cultivation that is destroying huge tracts of forest. Agroforestry involves harvesting produce from forest trees and shrubs usually without felling or harming them, and is therefore sustainable.

Extractive reserves

In 1990, the Brazilian government passed laws granting more than 2 million hectares (5 million acres) of rainforest to be managed for agroforestry. These forests are called extractive reserves. Local people manage them, harvesting produce such as fruit, nuts, palm oil, and medicinal plants. Tree sap called latex is tapped to make rubber. Rubber tapping is an industry in the Amazon that dates back to the early 20th century. Extractive reserves were the brainchild of green activist and rubber tapper Chico Mendes (see panel).

Legal recognition of local peoples' rights to make a living from sustainable farming is important. In the past, indigenous (native) peoples were often forced off lands by loggers, miners, and ranchers. This was possible because, despite the fact that their ancestors had lived there for centuries, they had no legal rights to the land. The loggers, miners, and ranchers then exploited and removed natural resources. Now the work of activists such as Chico Mendes has convinced the governments of some Amazon nations that granting land to indigenous peoples presents the best chance of preserving the forest. In 1990, the Colombian government signed over half of all its land in the Amazon to local peoples for this reason.

"At first I thought I was fighting to save rubber trees, then I thought I was fighting to save the Amazon rainforest. Now I realize I am fighting for humanity."

Chico Mendes

Chico Mendes: green hero

Chico Mendes (1944–88) was a Brazilian rubber tapper, trades union leader, and green activist who fought to preserve the Amazon rainforest, and also for education and workers' rights. Mendes helped to unite rubber tappers throughout Brazil into a national organization. He called on the Brazilian government to recognize the rights of rubber tappers and halt deforestation. He also called for government support for sustainable forestry and an end to subsidies for forest clearance. His campaigns made him internationally famous, but they also made him an enemy of the cattle barons who were clearing the Amazon for ranching. In 1988, Mendes was assassinated. Following widespread protests, the Brazilian government launched an investigation and eventually convicted a cattle baron of his murder.

Harvesting produce such as fruits, nuts, and rubber sustainably keeps rainforest ecosystems intact, and protects the forest soil, natural cycles, and biodiversity. Research shows that forest land that is managed for agroforestry yields far more profit per hectare than land that is cleared for agriculture or even felled for timber. What's more, the forest remains productive for decades, creating a much more long-term source of income than either logging or ranching.

Extractive reserves cover one per cent of the Amazon and provide a living for 63,000 families of rubber tappers.

ENVIRONMENTALISM IN ACTION

Greening the Dust Bowl

The Great Plains in the heart of North America has been settled and farmed since the 19th century. However, in the 1930s poor farming practices combined with years of dry weather brought environmental and economic disaster to the region.

What caused the Dust Bowl?

In the early 1900s, the desire to cut costs and increase production drove US farmers on the Great Plains to use practices that harmed the soil. Low crop prices led farmers into debt, forcing them to put new, drought-prone land under cultivation, or convert it to pasture. Crops were planted that were unsuitable to the region's light soil and harsh climate, with strong winds and low rainfall. In particular, wheat was planted year after year without allowing the land to lie fallow, which would have helped restore fertility. Above all, deep ploughing using the one-way disc plough removed deep-rooted grasses that had held the soil together and trapped moisture. All this made the land vulnerable to erosion.

Drought and erosion

In the 1930s the region was hit by unusually dry weather, with bad droughts in 1930–31 and 1934–37. High winds picked up loose soil and blew it away in "black blizzards". The region lost an estimated 75 per cent of its valuable topsoil, much of which was carried far east and ended up in the Atlantic Ocean. Some 400,000 square kilometres (154,440 square miles) of farmland in Texas, Oklahoma, and neighbouring states became a barren "dust bowl". Thousands of farming families, around half the region's population, were forced to leave the Midwest. Most moved west to earn a meagre living as fruit-pickers. Many would have starved without welfare handouts.

Recovery

Farming in the American Midwest took decades to recover. It did so through the introduction of farming practices that gradually restored the soil. The US president, Franklin D. Roosevelt, ordered belts of trees to be planted from Canada to Texas to provide windbreaks to shelter crops. Reservoirs were enlarged and new ones were built. Irrigation and water supplies were improved. In the early 1930s, the US government set up the Soil Conservation Service (SCS) to educate farmers about soil conservation methods, and fund them to use them.

Modern times

In modern times, the American Midwest continues to produce abundant harvests of cereals such as corn, wheat, and oats, living up to its reputation as the nation's "breadbasket". It is, however, one of the most intensively farmed areas in North America, with less than one per cent of the original grassland remaining.

"Black blizzards" darkened prairie skies for weeks during the Dust Bowl era.

THE FOOD INDUSTRY

The last 60 years have seen huge changes not only in farming, but also in the way that food is processed, transported, and sold to reach our tables. These changes have important economic and social consequences – and far-reaching effects for the natural world.

Nowadays, supermarkets offer a huge range of products – not just food. Many people do all their shopping in supermarkets. They can even order it online and have it delivered. Supermarkets save shoppers time and energy and are extremely convenient. The biggest supermarkets are huge multinational corporations that wield immense power over both shoppers and suppliers. In the United Kingdom, the top five supermarkets control 70 per cent of the grocery trade. The US supermarket chain Walmart is the world's top retailer, exceeding even the largest oil companies in turnover.

Then and Now
The rise of supermarkets

Seventy years ago, people shopped at specialist local shops and markets for their bread, meat, and groceries. The first supermarkets opened in the 1950s and became increasingly popular in later decades. Today, people in developed countries do 80 per cent of their shopping at supermarkets which offer a vast range of foods from all over the world.

Pressure on farmers and communities

In an effort to increase their share of trade, supermarkets regularly undercut one another's prices. This is good for shoppers but makes things difficult for farmers, both in developing countries and in the developed world. Since the 1980s, many European farmers have been forced out of business by the ultra-low prices supermarkets offer for their food.

Supermarkets also set very high standards for the food they buy. Fruit and vegetables that are not of an exact size and shape, or free of all blemishes, are often rejected. This leads to enormous waste.

Supermarket requirements also encourage farmers to use more chemicals to product perfect goods, which harms the environment. However, pressure from environmentalists has meant that regulations and standards have been slightly relaxed recently.

Supermarkets compete with one another through price wars, and by pursuing an aggressive policy of opening new stores. These huge stores generally cover large areas, often resulting in habitat loss on the edge of towns. Environmental groups say that the huge amounts of energy needed for lighting, heating, cooling, and freezing in supermarket premises produce vast quantities of greenhouse gases.

New supermarkets also have social and economic consequences for local communities, particularly in country areas. Many local shops find it impossible to compete with the prices and range offered by supermarkets, and go out of business. One official study estimated that the opening of a supermarket triggered the closure of all village shops within a 11-kilometre (7-mile) radius. However, the opening of large stores helps to provide jobs for the local community.

"Some 65,000 people left farming between 1996 and 2002. Eighteen thousand jobs in agriculture were lost in 2002 alone."

National Farmers' Union, UK

The fresh produce section in supermarkets reflects the vast range of groceries that are sold by the major retail chains.

Food packaging

Since the 1990s, green organizations have highlighted the waste disposal problem caused by the vast amounts of packaging generated by supermarkets and fast food outlets. In developed countries, at least 20 per cent of all household waste is food packaging, with each US citizen generating 2.1 kilograms (5½ pounds) of waste a day.

For years, environmental groups have pointed out that manufacturers and supermarkets use packaging not only to protect and preserve goods, but also to make them look attractive, to encourage people to buy. In the 1980s and 1990s, the volume of food packaging increased greatly, despite the fact that lighter materials were being used to reduce weight.

Waste disposal

By the 1990s, the sheer volume of supermarket packaging was presenting a major waste disposal problem worldwide. Most waste in the developed world was deposited in landfill sites, but if not properly sealed, these could cause soil and water pollution. Space for landfill sites was also running out in many European countries. Waste was also incinerated (burned), but environmentalists warned that this led to harmful air pollution. Green groups pointed out that while packaging such as cardboard **biodegraded** (decayed) relatively quickly, plastic packaging took hundreds of years to decay, and glass bottles did not biodegrade.

Environmentalists warned that food packaging was presenting a serious environmental hazard. The manufacture of packaging was not only a waste of valuable materials such as timber and minerals, but was also using vast amounts of energy and releasing greenhouse gases. The only plus was that the manufacturing of packaging created tens of thousands of jobs worldwide.

Reducing packaging

Green groups worldwide launched a drive to reduce waste. They urged people to follow "the 3 Rs" of waste reduction: reduce, reuse, and recycle. The campaign became widely popular in the 1990s, as consumers in many countries began to recycle and avoid over-packaged goods. People put pressure on supermarkets to reduce packaging or use biodegradable materials. Supermarkets were urged to find alternatives to plastic bags, which were singled out as particularly harmful and wasteful. At the same time, governments introduced recycling schemes, such as bottle banks and roadside collection schemes, to reduce the volume of waste that went to landfill.

Anti-packaging protests

The Women's Institute (WI) is the largest voluntary organization for women in the United Kingdom. In 2006, the WI launched a day of action against supermarket packaging. The aim was to highlight the harmful environmental impact and demand a change in supermarket policy. In over 100 locations, WI members returned excess packaging to supermarkets, forcing them to take notice. A day of action by such an established organization showed how much green thinking had caught on with the general public.

In the first decade of the 21st century, supermarkets and other food outlets responded to public and government pressure to reduce packaging. Many supermarkets stopped giving away free plastic bags and encouraged customers to use reusable bags. Biodegradable plastic bags, which will break down after a time when composted or buried in landfills, were developed by scientists – an example of biotechnology providing career openings and a highly saleable product. Nowadays, most people in developed countries recycle and support the drive to reduce packaging. In the United States, both cloth and paper grocery bags are widely used, while in European countries many more shoppers are using cloth bags again.

Cloth bags that can be used many times help to reduce the vast numbers of plastic bags that are discarded, creating a waste disposal problem.

Food miles

Seventy years ago, grocery shops in developed countries mainly stocked locally grown fruit and vegetables that were in season. There was relatively little imported produce on sale. Today, supermarkets offer shoppers a vast range of items, including tropical produce. Much of this food is transported thousands of kilometres by ship, plane, train, and truck. One US study estimated that a carrot travels an average of 2,957 kilometres (1,838 miles) to reach the dinner table. Food imports to developed countries increased following World War II, and grew very rapidly in the late 20th century. For example, food imports into the United Kingdom nearly trebled in the 20 years between 1980 and 2000.

Since the 1990s, environmental groups have highlighted the environmental cost of "food miles" – the distance food travels from the point of origin to shops and supermarkets. They have pointed out that food miles are a major source of greenhouse gases. According to environmental experts, food transport in the United Kingdom now totals a staggering 30 billion kilometres per year, and food production is responsible for 20 per cent of all greenhouse gases.

Reducing food miles

In the 1990s, discussion of food miles fed into widespread concern about climate change. Countries worldwide met to agree targets to reduce greenhouse gas emissions, and many passed laws requiring factories, farming, and food suppliers to reduce carbon emissions. Yielding to pressure from governments and consumers, supermarkets and food traders introduced measures to reduce food miles. For example, transport companies lowered truck speeds to conserve energy. Some supermarkets use advanced IT technology to plan vehicle journeys to reduce emissions – another example of green technology creating jobs and careers.

Supermarkets are also required to label products with the country of origin. However, one US study of the total carbon footprint of food production found that transportation was of minor importance compared to emissions from agricultural chemicals and the energy used by farm and food processing machinery.

Journeys to supermarkets

Environmentalists say that the out-of-town locations of many supermarkets (requiring a special car journey) also add to carbon emissions.

About one in ten car journeys in the United Kingdom are for food shopping – and more frequent car use adds to air pollution. Supermarkets argue that the growth of online shopping has reduced vehicle journeys. One van delivering groceries to many locations uses less fuel than many car trips.

Buying locally

As part of the drive to reduce greenhouse gases, environmental groups argue for a return to more locally sourced foods, urging people to buy locally grown foods from outlets such as farm shops, farmers' markets, and community farming projects. As well as reducing food miles, this supports local farmers and can help to regenerate local economies. Thanks to the work of campaign groups, many people now make more effort to buy local foods, or even grow their own food. Many people now check supermarket food labels for the country of origin, and favour locally sourced foods.

Shoppers who buy locally produced fruit and vegetables at farmers' markets are helping to reduce the air pollution produced by food miles.

A new approach to food production

Environmentalists are now calling for reforms in the way the food industry is run and regulated to give farmers as well as consumers a fairer deal. Groups such as Friends of the Earth call for the creation of supermarket watchdogs that would oversee prices and make sure supermarkets deal fairly with small shops and suppliers. They call on governments to make supermarkets more accountable for their impact on local communities, and do more to support rural communities.

Environmentalists call on supermarkets to reduce pollution and waste by cutting food miles, using less packaging, and increasing their support for locally grown foods, organic foods, and fair trade produce.

Environmentally friendly supermarkets

In the early 2000s, many supermarkets responded to pressure from green groups and the general public by announcing a new commitment to environmentally friendly food production. For example, in 2007 the supermarket Tesco announced plans to deliver a "revolution in green consumption". In 2011, Tesco announced it was "championing sustainable living" by investing £125 million in researching new ways to reduce carbon emissions and developing renewable energies.

> "In recent months a green tidal wave has washed down the high street, with retailers falling over themselves to chase the climate-friendly pound, and to buff up their corporate PR credentials in the process."
>
> Writer Mark Lynas, 2007

The supermarket chain Marks and Spencer has gone further than most to affirm its commitment to the environment. In 2007, it announced its "Plan A" to remodel its stores on environmentally friendly lines. Plan A made a total of 100 environmental commitments. These included a pledge to recycle or compost all food waste instead of sending it to landfill, and a commitment to become carbon neutral by 2012 by increasing energy savings and sustainable energy use. In 2011, it announced that its campaign had already achieved notable successes: its stores were now 10 per cent more energy-efficient, its transportation was 20 per cent more fuel-efficient, its food packaging had been reduced by 18 per cent, and food carrier-bag use was down by 83 per cent.

Distribution centres take up a lot of land, which can result in habitat loss. This is a Walmart distribution centre in the central United States.

Criticisms of "green" claims

While green groups may feel much of this commitment is genuine, they are wary of some environmental claims made by supermarkets, fast-food chains, and other businesses. Some green commentators have accused companies of "**greenwashing**" – making misleading use of terms coined by green activists to suggest that the company's aim is to be environmentally friendly. Like all businesses, supermarkets are mainly driven by the desire to make a profit, which is why they respond to public pressure. Some green writers are critical of supermarket publicity that implies that "all we need to do to save the planet is shop". Green activist George Monbiot has written: "Green consumerism will not save the biosphere. No political challenge can be met by shopping". On the plus side, all genuine actions taken by supermarkets to support sustainable farming and food production is good news for the environment.

FEAST AND FAMINE

Over the last 50 years, farming and food production have been industrialized in an effort to keep pace with the world's rising population. Farmers around the world have succeeded in producing enough food for all the people on the planet. However, changing diets and inequalities in food distribution mean that millions of people are still hungry.

Surpluses and overeating

In the developed world, intensive farming since the 1950s has made agriculture super-efficient, producing food surpluses. Fruit or vegetable "mountains" and milk "lakes" occur quite regularly in Europe and North America, with large quantities of food being dumped because it cannot be sold. The high standards demanded by supermarkets means that "imperfect" produce is often wasted.

Experts estimate that 27 per cent of all food in the United States is wasted somewhere along the food chain, either on farms, during transport, in supermarkets, or by consumers themselves. A recent survey in the United Kingdom found that up to 40 per cent of all vegetables and salad foods is wasted. Unfortunately, the high costs of transport and the relatively short shelf life of fruit and vegetables mean that very little of these surpluses can be used to feed hungry people in developing countries.

In Western nations, so much food is available at relatively cheap prices that overeating is now a serious problem. Experts say that over half the population in the United Kingdom, Germany, and the United States is overweight. **Obesity** leads to health problems such as heart disease, strokes, and diabetes. It kills at least 250,000 people in the United States each year. Meanwhile, in less developed countries, millions are starving. In 2010, the FAO estimated that around 925 million people were hungry – that's almost 1 in 7.

Measuring hunger

Malnutrition (not getting enough nourishment) can be measured by comparing the average **calorie** intake among people in different countries. Calories measure the energy you get from food. Health experts say people need an average of 2,250 calories a day. People in some parts of Africa get less than 1,600 calories a day. Meanwhile, in the West, the average intake is over 3,200 calories.

Causes of famine

In developing regions such as Africa and Asia, famine can be caused by drought, floods, cyclones, or wars. Bad farming practices such as overgrazing can turn productive land into deserts. However, experts say the main cause of hunger is poverty, because the very poor do not have the money to buy food or the land to grow it. Aid agencies supply millions of tonnes of food relief to famine victims, but say it is also vital to provide the economic aid to put famine-stricken communities back on their feet.

Changing diets

In the last 20 or 30 years, diets have changed quite dramatically in many parts of the world. Studies by food experts show that as developing countries industrialize, people move to a more Western-style diet. This includes junk foods and other processed foods that are high in salt, sugar, and fat. In nations such as China and India, changing diets have resulted in an increase in the health problems that plague Western nations, such as diabetes, obesity, and tooth decay.

This pie chart shows the number of hungry people in the world, by region.

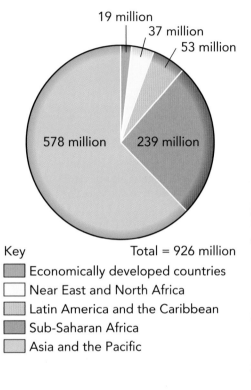

19 million
37 million
53 million
578 million
239 million

Total = 926 million

Key
- Economically developed countries
- Near East and North Africa
- Latin America and the Caribbean
- Sub-Saharan Africa
- Asia and the Pacific

A food "mountain" – large numbers of surplus tomatoes are dumped on a farm in the Canary Islands.

ENVIRONMENTALISM IN ACTION

Meaty diets

The main change to diets in developing regions such as Asia and South America in the last 30 or 40 years has been a dramatic increase in the consumption of meat and dairy produce. Meat consumption in Japan rose by an amazing 360 per cent between 1960 and 1990, partly replacing traditional sources of protein such as fish. People in China ate an average of 20 kilograms (44 pounds) of meat per year in 1980, but that had risen to 52 kilograms (114 pounds) per year by 2008. In India, meat consumption rose by 40 per cent in the 15 years between 1992 and 2007.

These figures are still low compared to meat consumption in the West. The average European eats 74 kilograms (163 pounds) of meat per year, while the average for the United States is 125 kilograms (275 pounds). Environmentalists say that if everyone on Earth ate as much meat as we do in developed nations, several planets would be needed to support all the livestock.

Health issues

According to the FAO, meat production quadrupled between 1960 and 2008, while the world population doubled. According to doctors, high meat and dairy consumption leads to health problems such as heart disease, strokes, and some cancers – and these problems are increasing in Asia. Although meat is an excellent source of protein, the World Health Organization (WHO) believes that people in the West are eating far more protein than is good for them.

Straining natural resources

Environmentalists point out that increasing meat consumption worldwide is damaging ecosystems and putting added pressure on overstretched natural resources, such as water supplies and arable land. Scientists calculate that livestock farming already occupies 70 per cent of all farmland, and 30 per cent of Earth's land surface. Rising meat consumption will increase world hunger because an even greater percentage of all crops that are grown will be used to feed animals, not people.

Livestock currently consume 40 per cent of the world's grain harvest, and growing crops such as soybeans for fodder is contributing to deforestation in places like the Amazon. The world's livestock also consume 15 per cent of all irrigated water. Meanwhile, 2 billion people worldwide suffer from water shortages. Environmental studies suggest that if livestock farming continues to increase, it could take up to half of the world's irrigated water by 2025.

Eating less meat

Environmental scientists and other food experts conclude that modern intensive livestock farming is inefficient and unsustainable. They calculate that land used to support beef cattle to feed 10 people could feed 300 people if planted with maize. Groups such as Greenpeace are calling on people in the West to consume less meat and dairy produce, and for governments to support livestock farmers to move towards lower-input methods, such as raising cattle on grass rather than specially grown fodder.

However, despite these warnings, global meat consumption continues to rise steadily, with the biggest increases occurring in developing countries. The Worldwatch Institute predicts that global meat consumption will double by 2050.

Cattle graze on deforested land in the Amazon. Cattle ranching is the biggest cause of deforestation in Brazil.

Fish stocks and overfishing

Fish and shellfish have sustained people living on coasts, lakes, and rivers since prehistoric times. For centuries, fishing was done on a small scale. It did not harm fish stocks since they were naturally replenished through breeding. However, in the 20th century, fishing developed on an industrial scale. Technology, such as sonar, and huge nets stretching for kilometres made commercial fishing fleets super-efficient. This is sometimes called the "Blue Revolution". Between 1950 and 1990, the world's total fish catch rose steeply, from less than 20 million tonnes a year to over 70 million tonnes.

Today, some 90 million tonnes of fish are netted annually worldwide. Of this, over 40 per cent is traded internationally. Amazingly, nearly half of the total catch is processed into fishmeal to feed farm livestock. Over 20 million tonnes is by-catch – species such as sharks, dolphins, seabirds, and turtles – that fishermen do not want. It is simply thrown back, mostly dead.

Marine monitoring organizations say that 75 per cent of the world fish stocks are now dwindling because they are overfished. Fish populations in many lakes and rivers are also severely depleted. In 2002, the world's fishing nations agreed to reduce their fish catches by setting limits called quotas. Marine conservation groups recommend that the total world catch should be reduced even further, to allow fish stocks to recover. Environmentalists recommend only eating fish species that are still plentiful or that are caught from sustainable stocks.

Is fish farming the answer?

Aquaculture, or fish farming, is often recommended as a way of conserving wild fish stocks. In 2005, fish and shellfish farming produced 48 million tonnes of food. However, environmental groups such as Greenpeace argue that aquaculture harms marine ecosystems in several different ways. Not only are wild fish caught to feed farmed fish, but disease can also spread from farmed fish to wild stocks. Shrimp farming, which involves the creation of ponds by the shore, also damages coastal habitats such as mangrove swamps, which act as nurseries for wild fish populations.

Dolphin-friendly tuna

Fishermen have long known that ocean-dwelling tuna are often found near schools of dolphins. In the 1950s, Pacific fishing fleets began to catch tuna by chasing and surrounding dolphins in purse-seine nets. Thousands of dolphins were routinely trapped and killed. Over the next 40 years, an estimated 7 million dolphins died. In 1986, the International Marine Mammal Project called for shoppers to stop buying tuna caught in this way. A video showing dolphins dying in the tuna nets shocked audiences worldwide.

The boycott was effective. In 1990, the three largest tuna companies agreed to end the dolphin-deadly practice and adopt safer methods. The "dolphin-safe" label was introduced on cans to distinguish tuna caught using dolphin-friendly methods. Thanks to the campaign, the numbers of dolphins killed yearly fell from over 80,000 to under 3,000. However, Greenpeace has recently voiced criticism of even dolphin-friendly tuna fishing. Tuna stocks are now dangerously low, and dolphin-friendly methods do not prevent the death of other by-catch, such as seabirds and turtles.

Fishermen unload a catch of Pacific tuna on an island in Micronesia. Some species of tuna, such as bluefin, are endangered by overfishing.

Feeding the world

Between 1960 and 2000, the world population doubled from 3 billion to 6 billion, placing enormous pressure on farming. However, experts say the amount of food available per person actually increased by about one-fifth during the same time. Clearly, the world's farmers are able to provide enough food for everyone, but the problem is that food distribution is very unequal.

Developed countries, which make up just 30 per cent of the world's population, get around 60 per cent of the food. This leaves the developing world with massive food shortages. According to the FAO, up to 2 billion people – nearly one-third of the world's population – mostly living in poor countries, are hungry or malnourished. Moreover, populations are rising fastest on continents such as Africa, South America, and Asia, where good farmland is scarce and poverty and famine are widespread.

Environmentalists believe that the modern food industry and international trade agreements are adding to problems of poverty and famine in the developing world, not helping to solve them. They argue that intensive farming and the current "free trade" system favour developed nations at the expense of the developing world. This is increasing debt in poor countries.

In many developing countries, the large food corporations are pushing small farmers off their land. The most productive land is given over to grow cash crops for the West and pay off international debts. In countries such as India, a high percentage of crops are earmarked for the West, while local people are starving. Environmentalists and others call for international trade agreements to be revised to provide a fairer deal for small-scale farmers in the developing world.

A new food economy

Governments, international agencies, and aid charities provide food aid and loans to ease famine in regions such as Africa. These measures help to ease hunger in the short term. However, environmental experts say the real solution is to enable poor countries to become self sufficient in food, not dependent on Western aid. This issue is called **food security** or **food sovereignty**.

Environmentalists believe that investment in agriculture is an important part of working towards **food security**. The money should be invested, not in intensive farming with its reliance on expensive machinery and chemicals, but in sustainable agriculture, which is most suited to farming in areas with scant water and poor soil. Resources and training are needed to encourage good farming practices that will improve the soil, conserve water supplies, and protect the environment. Environmentalists believe that, in this way, sustainable farming offers the best hope for food security and an end to hunger.

Improvements in healthcare and sanitation, along with education in hygiene, nutrition, and family planning, will also help to improve living standards. Studies show that when living standards rise, the population rate falls naturally, as it has in the developed world. This will also help to ease famine.

"The solution lies not in feeding the world but allowing the world to feed itself."

Greenpeace

Water pours into a new reservoir in Senegal in West Africa. This irrigation project was funded by development money.

LOOKING INTO THE FUTURE

In 2011, the world population reached 7 billion. By 2040, there may well be over 9 billion people on the planet. Over the next decades, the world's farmers will continue to face the challenge of feeding everyone, while coping with new problems, such as climate change. Does intensive farming provide the way forward, or, as environmentalists claim, is sustainable farming the only way to feed the world without sacrificing the Earth?

Impact of global warming

Scientists are using some of the world's most sophisticated computers to predict the effects of global warming. The predictions are that rising temperatures will make weather patterns generally more extreme. Areas that are already dry, such as Australia and Africa, are likely to experience more droughts, while areas prone to floods may get wetter. Storms will probably become more common, and hurricanes more intense. Events such as the recent droughts in Australia suggest that climate change may already be taking effect.

Sea levels are rising as the oceans warm and polar ice melts. In future, rising sea levels will threaten large areas of farmland in low-lying countries such as Bangladesh and the Netherlands. All of this will make farming more difficult. Scientists suggest that the world's farmlands may have to expand into wilderness areas to meet growing demands for food, causing more habitat loss.

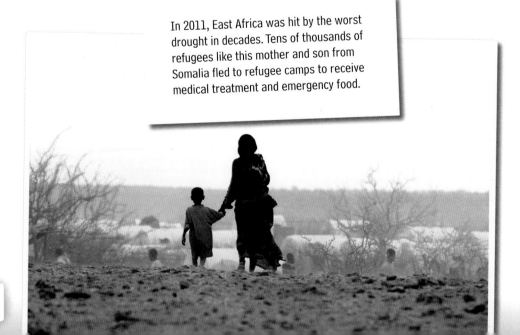

In 2011, East Africa was hit by the worst drought in decades. Tens of thousands of refugees like this mother and son from Somalia fled to refugee camps to receive medical treatment and emergency food.

Winners and losers

Climate change may well bring winners as well as losers. Cold places such as Russia and northern Canada may become more suitable for farming. However, environmentalists fear that the world's poorest farmers, in regions such as Africa, are likely to be among the hardest hit. What's more, poor countries have fewer resources to combat the effects of climate change.

Tackling climate change

At the 1997 climate conference in Kyoto, Japan, many nations agreed to reduce greenhouse gas emissions by 5 per cent by 2012. However, little progress has been made since then. Talks stalled at the Copenhagen conference in 2009, with delegates failing to agree the cuts needed to keep the increase in average global temperature below 2°C (3.6°F) for fear of damaging their economies.

Environmentalists say more radical greenhouse gas cuts are urgently needed to minimize the effects of climate change and protect the world's farmlands, ecosystems, and wildlife. Green groups urge governments to invest more in renewable technologies that provide an alternative to fossil fuels. They also call on each and every one of us to reduce our carbon footprint by using energy more carefully. Thanks to green campaigns worldwide, and also rising fuel costs, many people are now reducing their energy consumption through such measures as using cars less, and public transport more.

Biofuels

Crops such as soybeans, maize, and oilseed rape can be used to fuel cars, as an alternative to carbon-producing petrol and diesel. These crops are now being farmed in greater quantities to meet rising fuel demands. However, every field that is sown with biofuel crops means that less land is available to grow food. The land needed to grow biofuel to fill the tank of a large car just once could feed a person for a year. Many experts say growing crops for biofuel will make it even more difficult to grow enough food for everyone.

ENVIRONMENTALISM IN ACTION

Who owns the world's seeds?

Scientists in favour of genetic modification claim that biotechnology will help to solve the problem of hunger in a warming world, by creating crops that can resist drought, grow in thin soil, or contain extra vitamins. However, many people worry that claiming ownership of crops, as the biotech companies are doing, could put added pressure on farmers and even threaten food security.

Seed patents

GM seeds are developed and manufactured by large and powerful transnational companies (TNCs). These companies assert their ownership over the GMOs, or modified crops, by taking out patents. A patent is a legal claim to ownership of an invention or piece of technology, so others cannot use, make, or sell it. The GMOs developed by the biotech companies have been patented. Farmers wishing to buy seeds for these modified crops must sign a contract agreeing not to save seeds from the harvest to sow in future years. Instead, they have to buy new seeds every year. Farmers who break the contract are sued and face heavy fines.

In the first decade of the 21st century, many environmental groups launched campaigns to publicize what they saw as the dangers of seed patenting. Environmentalists say farmers have been saving seeds for at least 11,000 years, and no one should be allowed to claim ownership over a natural product. But the biotech companies say GM crops would not have occurred naturally.

"Life science" companies

The companies that are developing GMOs mostly started out as manufacturers of farm chemicals. In the 1990s, they moved into the seed market by buying up seed suppliers worldwide. Now calling themselves "life science companies", just a handful of TNCs based in the USA or Europe now control over 50 per cent of the world's seed market. They also dominate the pesticides industry.

Environmental groups and many other people worry that dominance of the world seed market has made the large biotech companies extremely powerful. Critics fear that they influence government policies and trade agreements, effectively holding the world to ransom. Environmentalists worry that if crops fail, poor farmers would not be able to buy fresh seeds, which would threaten future harvests. They believe that by controlling the range of seeds that are on the market, TNCs can effectively control what farmers grow, threatening food security.

Threatening biodiversity

Environmentalists also worry that dominance of the seed market by a few companies is reducing the total number of crops that are grown, and so threatening biodiversity. For example, Indian farmers once grew 30,000 varieties of rice. Now 75 per cent of the rice crop is planted with just a dozen varieties, increasing the risk of blight, disease, or pests wiping out harvests. The FAO is calling on farmers worldwide to save their seeds to preserve biodiversity. It is also investing in technology such as seed banks to preserve the variety of crops and plants.

"We oppose all patents on plants, animals and humans ... Life is not an industrial commodity."

Greenpeace

This is a genetically modified wheat crop growing in a field. Environmentalists say patenting GM crops poses a threat to food security worldwide.

What have we learned?

Environmentalists have made many people think much more about farming and its effects on the natural world, and about the food supply chain that transports food from distant continents to our homes. Campaigns about food and farming have inspired many people to do their bit in helping to protect the environment, and/or to join environmental groups. Concerns about the way our food is produced and delivered are now seldom out of the news.

In the past 20 or 30 years, green organizations have made many people aware of the problems that result from intensive farming. People now think more carefully about the threat to biodiversity and world food supplies that could be posed by overfishing or patenting GM crops. Green groups believe that modern intensive farming can only continue to feed the world at high cost to the environment. They believe that sustainable methods such as organic farming are the best way forward, because only sustainable farming will protect the environment on which we all depend for food.

Results and action

In recent years, environmentalists have influenced consumers' shopping habits. More people now think about how far foods have travelled when buying groceries from supermarkets. More people are visiting farm shops, markets, and other local outlets to buy locally grown foods, or buying organic and fair trade goods. The debate about GM crops has made consumers think about the ingredients in processed foods and about the future of farming. In many parts of the world, more people have started growing their own food, with demand for allotments on the rise.

Thanks to the work of green groups, people in Western nations are aware of the environmental impact and health risks of eating too much meat and dairy produce. Some people are eating less meat, while others only buy fish from sustainable sources. Many people are making more effort to eat a balanced, healthy diet.

In response to public pressure, many supermarkets are cutting waste, making food transport more fuel-efficient, and putting more locally grown foods on sale. In all these ways, environmentalism is now affecting what foods are available and how we think about food. Many people now believe that governments should give more support to sustainable farmers, both in developing and developed countries. Environmentalists say that if farmers are to continue to feed the world without damaging the planet in the process, a lot still needs to be achieved.

Thanks to the work of environmentalists, many people now shop carefully to find out where fresh produce is sourced and what goes into processed foods.

Millennium goals

At the Millennium Summit in 2000, the United Nations pledged to halve the number of people who are hungry and malnourished by 2015. Early in the decade, the UN reported progress had been made in Asia, Latin America, and the Caribbean. But by 2008, economic recession and high food prices were increasing poverty and hunger in many developing countries. According to the FAO, 824 million people were malnourished in 1990. By 2009, the figure was 1.02 billion. Environmentalists and aid organizations fear that too little has been done too late to reach the 2015 target.

TIMELINE

9000s BC First grain crops are cultivated by farmers in the Middle East and China. People begin rearing livestock around the same time.

c. **7000 BC** Rice cultivation begins in China.

c. **6000 BC** Farming begins in Egypt, Mexico, and the Indus Valley region.

4000–3000 BC A simple plough called the ard is invented in the Middle East.

c. **500 BC–AD 200** Farmers throughout the Roman Empire specialize in cultivating wheat, vines, and other crops, and practice crop rotation.

1700s Agricultural Revolution begins in Britain with the invention of the seed drill in 1701.

1831 US farmer Cyril McCormick invents the mechanical reaper.

1837 US blacksmith John Deere invents the steel plough, which is strong enough to cut roots, preparing the soil for cultivation.

c. **1850s** Steam-powered tractors are used on farms in Europe and the USA.

1866 Austrian monk Gregor Mendel publishes a paper explaining how inheritance works, which helps farmers develop new crop varieties and breeds of livestock.

1874 The invention of barbed wire in the USA allows ranchlands to be fenced.

1920s All-purpose tractors are in use on farms in Europe and the USA.

1930–1940 Drought and bad farming practices turn the North American prairie into a dust bowl, causing widespread hardship.

1930s Artificial fertilizers are used on farms in developed countries.

1935 The Soil Conservation Act is passed in the USA.

1939 Swiss chemist Paul Müller discovers the insecticidal properties of DDT.

1945 The United Nations Food and Agriculture Organization (FAO) is founded.

1945–1970 Advances in farming technology such as high-yield varieties (HYVs) lead to increased food production in developed countries.

1950s The first supermarkets open in the USA and Europe.

1957 The European Economic Community (EEC, later the European Union, EU) is founded. Its Common Agricultural Policy is launched, with the aim of modernizing farming in Europe.

1960s Fair trade movement is launched in Europe, becoming increasingly influential from the 1970s. HYVs are introduced to developing countries – the "Green Revolution".

1961 The World Wildlife Fund (WWF) is founded for the conservation, research, and restoration of the natural environment.

1962 Rachel Carson's book *Silent Spring* is published, describing the harmful effects of DDT.

1969 The environmental group Friends of the Earth is founded.

1970 The first Earth Day is held in the USA to inspire awareness of Earth's natural environment.

1971 The international environmental organization Greenpeace is founded in Canada, and later spreads worldwide.

1972 The US Environmental Protection Agency bans most uses of DDT.

1974 Chinese scientists create the first hybrid rice, which is soon increasing rice harvests worldwide.

1977 US Soil and Water Resources Conservation Act is passed.

1980s The new science of biotechnology improves crops and livestock.

1985 Rainforest Action Network (RAN) is founded to protect rainforests worldwide.

1987 RAN calls for a boycott of the fast-food chain Burger King, which is importing cheap beef from deforested land in South America.

1988 Assassination of green activist and rubber tapper Chico Mendes.

1990 Dolphin-safe label introduced on cans of tuna.

1992 The United Nations Conference on Environment and Development, also known as the Earth Summit, is held in Rio de Janeiro, Brazil. It achieves progress in limiting greenhouse gases that are producing climate change.

1994 The first genetically modified food crop is released onto the market.

1997 At the climate conference in Kyoto, Japan, many countries commit to reducing their greenhouse gas emissions, but the USA does not.

2000 United Nations pledges to halve the number of people who are hungry by 2015.

2004 Stockholm Conference bans the use of DDT in farming.

2005 Environmental Stewardship Scheme (ESS) is launched in the UK. Lasers replace stickers on food labels in supermarkets.

2006 Women's Institute in the UK organizes anti-packaging protest in 100 supermarkets.

2008 The Climate Conference in Copenhagen achieves little progress in reducing greenhouse gases.
The FAO becomes a major force for improvements in agriculture worldwide, with 191 member-states.

GLOSSARY

Agricultural Revolution period of rapid development in farming that started in the 1700s

agrochemicals chemicals used in farming, such as fertilizers and insecticides

agroforestry harvesting of produce from trees or shrubs

antibiotic drug used to cure disease caused by bacteria in either people and animals. Overuse of antibiotics can lead bacteria to develop resistance to these drugs.

aquifer layer of rock which holds water

biodegrade decay

biodiversity variety of life in a particular habitat

biofuel fuel made from natural materials, such as crops or plant waste

biotechnology use of biological processes or living things to manufacture products. Genetic engineering is a form of biotechnology.

calorie unit of energy

cash crop crop that is grown for money, usually for export

crop rotation the practice of changing the crops that are grown in fields from year to year

deforestation when forest land is cleared of trees

deplete use up or exhaust a resource

desertification when land becomes infertile due to erosion or bad farming practices such as overgrazing

developed world countries of the world that are more socially and economically advanced than others

eco-friendly something that sustains the environment

ecosystem web of life made up of all the living things in a habitat together with the soil, air, and conditions such as climate

eutrophication when water becomes super-rich in nutrients which encourage algae

extensive farming method of farming which involves a low input from the farmer to gain a relatively low yield per hectare of land

fair trade movement movement to ensure farmers in developing countries get a fair price for their produce

fallow left uncultivated

feedlot plot of land where cattle are fattened for market

food security a nation's or a region's ability to feed itself

genes tiny structures inside the cells of living things that control inheritance

genetic engineering the process by which scientists alter the characteristics of living things by adding genes from different species

genetically modified (GM) created by genetic engineering

genetically modified organism (GMO) species or variety created by genetic engineering

global warming rising temperatures worldwide, caused by an increase of gases in the atmosphere that trap the Sun's heat

greenhouse gas gas that stores heat in the atmosphere. Carbon dioxide and methane are examples of greenhouse gases.

Green Revolution the research and spread of modern intensive agriculture to developing countries, which increased world harvests in the mid-1900s

greenwashing term coined by environmentalists to describe the activity of a business or practice that falsely claims it is sensitive to the environment

habitat place where particular living things normally live

high-yield variety (HYV) food crop developed to produce a large harvest

hormone chemical that regulates the working of cells or organs in animals, or controls a function, such as growth

intensive farming type of agriculture in which farmers use chemicals and modern machinery and methods to produce a high yield per hectare

intercrop grow several crops together in a field

legume plant belonging to the pea and bean family

lobby when people put pressure on politicians to try to influence them to vote in a certain way

monoculture growing the same crop year after year over a wide area

nutrient chemical that nourishes living things

obesity the condition of being seriously overweight

organic grown or produced without the use of chemical fertilizers and pesticides

organic farming method of farming without using chemical fertilizers and pesticides

pesticide chemical used to kill weeds, insects, or fungi that harm crops

renewable will not get used up

salinization when soil becomes too salty to grow crops

seed drill machine for sowing seeds

steppe vast grassy plain, found in eastern Europe and Siberia

subsidy grant or gift of money given by a government to a person or group in support of a business

subsistence farming when farmers are only able to grow enough food to feed their families, with little left over to sell

sustainable does not use up too many natural resources or pollute the environment

thresh separate grain from the stalks

winnow separate grain from the husks

FIND OUT MORE

Books

Conservation, Ian Rohr (A & C Black, 2007)

Farming, Jen Green (Wayland Publishers, 2011)

The GM Food Debate (Issues), Sophie Smiley (Independence Educational Publishers, 2007)

Environmental Activism (Protecting the Planet), Pamela Dell (Compass Point Books, 2010)

Sustainability and Environment (Issues), Cobi Smith (Independence Educational Publishers, 2008)

Sustaining Our Natural Resources (Environment Challenge), Jen Green (Raintree, 2011)

Websites

Websites about environmental protection

US Environment Protection Agency: **www.epa.gov**

Environment Agency UK: **www.environment-agency.gov.uk**

Department for Environment, UK: **www.defra.gov.uk**

Environment Protection Authority, Australia: **www.environment.gov.au**

The Young People's Trust for the Environment: a charity which aims to encourage young people's understanding of the environment and the need for sustainability: **www.ypte.org.uk**

Websites about food and farming

UN Food and Agriculture Organization: **www.fao.org**

wwf.panda.org/what_we_do/footprint/agriculture

wwf.panda.org/about_our_earth/teacher_resources/webfieldtrips/ sus_agriculture

wwf.panda.org/what_we_do/footprint/agriculture/impacts/soil_erosion

Friends of the Earth briefing on intensive livestock farming: **www.foe.co.uk/ resource/briefings/factory_farming.pdf**

Websites about sustainable and organic farming

The Soil Association: **www.soilassociation.org**

WWF briefing on sustainable farming:
  wwf.panda.org/what_we_do/footprint/agriculture

Friends of the Earth briefing on sustainable food:
  www.foe.co.uk/resource/briefings/eating_planet_briefing.pdf

Greenpeace briefing on the future of farming:
  www.greenpeace.org.uk/gm/the-future-of-agriculture

Websites about population and food

UN Food and Agriculture Organization: **www.fao.org**

United Nations Population Fund: **www.unpfa.org**

Friends of the Earth briefing on supermarkets:
  www.foe.co.uk/resource/briefings/checking_out_the_environme.pdf

Fairtrade UK: **www.fairtrade.org.uk**

Websites about deforestation

Rainforests: **rainforests.mongabay.com**

Rainforest Action Network, an environmental group which campaigns to
  protect rainforests worldwide: **ran.org**

WWF: **www.worldwildlife.org/what/wherewework/amazon/index.html**

Environmental organizations

Friends of the Earth: **www.foe.co.uk**

Greenpeace: **www.greenpeace.org**

WWF: **www.worldwildlife.org**

Sierra Club, USA: **www.sierraclub.org**

Topics to investigate

- Find out more about the fair trade movement:
  www.fairtrade.org.uk
- Find out more about the American Dust Bowl:
  www.drought.unl.edu/DroughtBasics/DustBowl.aspx
- Research into GM crops:
  www.citizenshipfoundation.org.uk/main/page.php?200
  www.independence.co.uk/shop/science-and-health/issues-today/gm-food

INDEX

Agricultural Revolution 8
agrochemicals 4, 10, 11,
  20–21, 26, 29, 40, 54
agroforestry 32–33
animal feed 24, 30, 47, 48
animal welfare issues 24
aquaculture 48

biodiversity 6, 11, 16, 18,
  25, 26, 28, 33, 55, 56
biofuels 18, 53
biotechnology 14, 39, 54

cash crops 12, 13, 50
climate change 7, 40,
  52–53
crop rotation 8, 30

deforestation 18, 19, 25,
  33, 47
desertification 23, 45
developed countries 4, 5,
  10, 12, 44, 50
developing countries 5, 11,
  12, 13, 44, 46, 47, 50
diets 5, 44, 45, 46–47
droughts 13, 45, 52
Dust Bowl 34–35

eco-friendly farming 17,
  26–29
ecosystems 11, 16, 17, 18,
  23, 26, 33, 46
environmentalism 4, 6–7,
  56
eutrophication 20

factory farming 24, 25
fair trade movement 13, 42
famine 11, 45, 50
fertilizers 10, 11, 18, 20,
  26, 29, 30
fish stocks 48–49
food industry 4, 36–43, 50
food miles 40, 41, 42

food security 50, 51
food surpluses 26, 44, 45
food waste 36, 42, 44

genetically modified (GM)
  crops 6, 14–15, 54, 55
global warming 7, 52
green movement see
  environmentalism
Green Revolution 11
greenhouse gases 7, 25,
  37, 38, 40, 53
greenwashing 43

habitat conservation and
  restoration 16–17, 19, 26,
  27, 28–29
habitat loss 4, 16, 17,
  25, 52
health issues 44, 45, 46
high-yield varieties (HYVs)
  10, 11, 20, 22

intensive farming 10, 16,
  18, 22, 24, 25, 26, 30,
  44, 50, 56
irrigation 11, 22, 23, 34,
  47, 51

livestock farming 24–25,
  30, 46–47
local communities 32, 33,
  37, 42
locally grown foods 4, 41,
  42, 56

malnutrition 44, 57
meat consumption 46–47,
  56
mechanization 8, 9, 10, 24,
  25, 26
Mendes, Chico 32, 33
monoculture 10
Muir, John 16, 17

national parks and reserves
  6, 17

organic farming 4, 30–31
overfishing 48
overgrazing 23, 45

packaging 38–39, 42
pesticides 4, 10, 11, 20–21,
  26, 54
pollution 4, 6, 20, 25,
  38, 41
population growth 10, 16,
  50, 52
poverty 45, 50, 53, 57

rainforests 16, 18–19, 32–3
renewable technologies 7,
  42, 53

salinization 22, 23
sea levels, rising 52
seed patenting 54–55
selective breeding 9, 14
soil erosion 23, 34
soybean cultivation 14, 16,
  23, 25, 47, 53
stewardship schemes 26,
  28–29
subsistence farming 10, 13
supermarkets 12, 36–43,
  56
sustainability 7, 30, 32, 42,
  51, 56

water use 11, 22–23, 47
wildlife 16, 17, 20, 21, 26,
  27, 28, 29, 48–49